EARTHQUAKES
and
VOLCANOES

Troll Associates

EARTHQUAKES
and
VOLCANOES

by Laurence Santrey

Illustrated by John Jones

Troll Associates

Library of Congress Cataloging in Publication Data

Santrey, Laurence.
    Earthquakes and volcanoes.

    Summary: Explains how earthquakes and volcanic
eruptions result from the building up of pressure
which begins far below the earth's surface.
    1. Earthquakes—Juvenile literature.
2. Volcanoes—Juvenile literature. [1. Earthquakes.
2. Volcanoes.   3. Earth] I. Jones, John R.
(John Ralph), 1935-   ill.   II. Title.
QE521.3.S26   1984   551.2′1   84-2676
ISBN 0-8167-0212-8 (lib. bdg.)
ISBN 0-8167-0213-6 (pbk.)

There is a rumbling in the earth. The ground trembles. A loud *bang* echoes across the hills. Suddenly a jagged crack appears and rips across the ground like a bolt of lightning. On one side of the crack, the ground pushes up, while the other side drops down. Trees snap in two, and huge boulders roll into the widening gap of land. At last, the quaking of the earth stops, but the earthquake has changed the landscape forever.

Far away, in another part of the world, a dormant volcano sleeps peacefully. Whitened by winter snows, its silent slopes are a beautiful sight beneath the clear blue sky.

Suddenly—without warning—clouds of black smoke billow up from the volcanic mountaintop. A deep, low roar grows louder and more threatening. And moments later, with a *boom* like a gigantic hammer

blow, the top of the mountain explodes, sending tons of rock hurtling into the air. Blistering hot molten lava pours from the fiery peak, as the volcano erupts in spectacular fury.

Earthquakes and erupting volcanoes have always been sources of wonder and terror. But until very recently, the reasons for these natural events were total mysteries, and people tried to explain them in many ways. To the ancient Greeks and Romans, volcanoes were the flaming furnaces of the god of fire. To the Polynesian people of the Pacific Ocean, volcanoes were signs of an angry goddess.

One of the Greek philosophers, Aristotle, thought that earthquakes were caused by winds trapped in underground caves. This idea—that certain kinds of weather were to blame for earthquakes—was believed by many people until modern times. Others were sure that earthquakes were the works of furious gods or of evil spirits.

When earthquakes shook New England in the eighteenth century, some Americans blamed Benjamin Franklin. They said that his invention, the lightning rod, set off the quakes by attracting electrical substances to earth.

Today, we know that volcanoes and earthquakes are not the actions of angry gods or the result of any other mysterious force. Rather, both are natural events that begin far below the earth's surface and are caused by pressure building up until it can't be held in any longer.

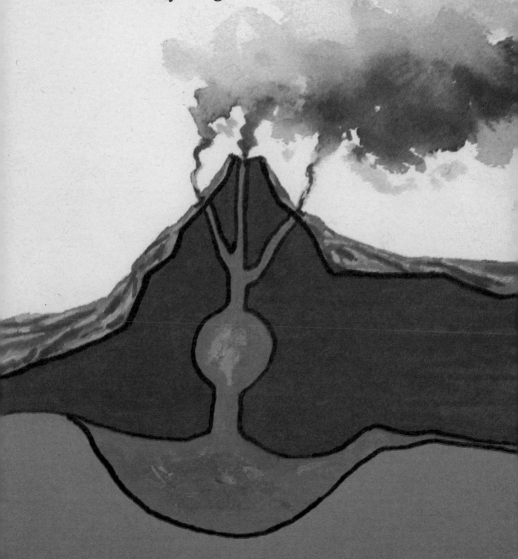

Scientists tell us that the part of the earth that we live on is just a thin crust of rock. Under this crust is a much thicker layer, called the mantle. The mantle is made up of hot, liquid rock known as magma. The crust is a hard cover over the mantle, but it is not one solid mass. Instead, it is made up of

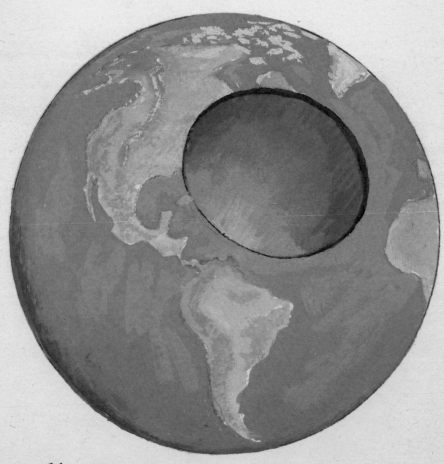

several huge pieces of rock called plates.

The plates are never completely motionless. In some places, two plates push against each other. In other places, two plates move away from each other. In still other places, two plates slowly slip past each other.

Plate

Plate

Along the length of the state of California, we can actually see where two plates meet. There, the North American plate meets the Pacific plate, forming the San Andreas Fault.

A fault is a break in the earth's crust. The city of San Francisco, in the northern part of the state, is built on the North American plate, near the fault line. And the city of Los Angeles, in the southern part of the state, is built on the Pacific plate, near the fault line. As these two plates slide past each other in opposite directions, they move at the rate of a few inches or centimeters a year. At this rate of movement, Los Angeles and San Francisco will be side by side in ten million years.

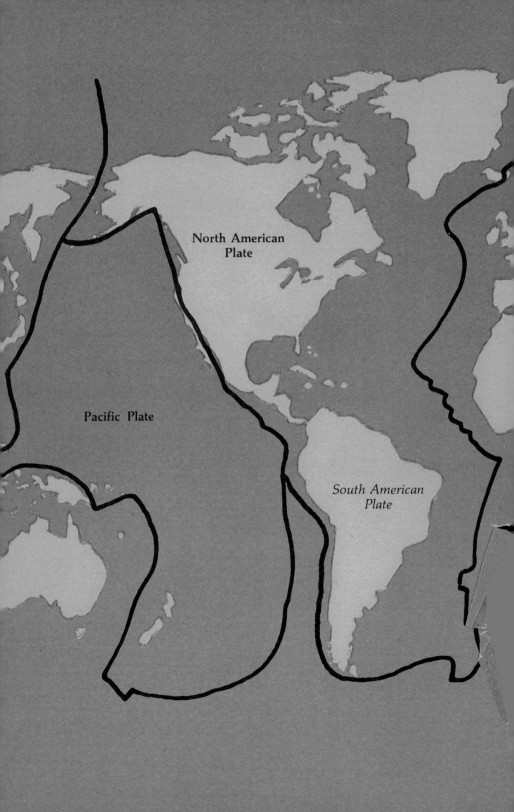

The shifting of the earth's plates is not smooth and even. In some places the edge of one plate may push under the edge of another plate. The two plates push and grind until the rocks can't take any more pressure. Then there is a sudden movement, known as an earthquake.

The force of an earthquake can be measured in two different ways. One way is by using the Richter scale. On the Richter scale, an earthquake of magnitude 1 can hardly be felt. Only a seismograph—a scientific instrument that measures the strength of a quake's shock waves—can measure a magnitude 1 quake.

A magnitude 2 quake is ten times stronger, and so on. Quakes of magnitude 1 through 4 are considered minor quakes. A quake of magnitude 5 causes local damage. Magnitude 6 is destructive of life and property. And anything beyond magnitude 7 is considered a major disaster.

One of the worst earthquakes on record struck Anchorage, Alaska in 1964. It measured over 8.5 on the Richter scale. The quake lasted three minutes, during which time buildings collapsed, streets dropped many feet, and homes were buried under landslides. The earthquake also raised or lowered the heights of some mountains and dropped the level of the nearby sea bottom.

This earthquake also created a huge wave of water known as a *tsunami*. The tsunami, a long, fast-moving wave, struck the city of Valdez, Alaska, many miles from Anchorage. Among its terrible effects were landslides, extensive property damage, and a number of deaths.

While the Alaskan quake registered 8.5 on the Richter scale, it measured 10 on the Modified Mercalli scale. The Mercalli scale grades earthquakes in terms of the damage they cause. On the Mercalli scale, a level-2 quake is barely felt. A level-4 quake causes cracks in walls, rattles dishes, and sounds like a truck driving into a wall. The really serious quakes start at level 8 and go through level 12. Anything over a 9 on the Mercalli scale is a quake of enormous magnitude.

Just as earthquakes occur along the edges of the Pacific plate, so do volcanoes. There are so many volcanoes along the western coast of North and South America, the southern coast of Alaska, and down the coast of Asia, that this line is called the "ring of fire."

Vent

Core

Magma
(molten rock)

Like an earthquake, an erupting volcano seems to be nature's way of easing underground pressure. But nobody knows exactly what sets off the eruption of magma, gases, steam, and ash that come pouring out of an active volcano. Volcanologists—people who study volcanoes—also do not know why some eruptions last for a day or a few days, while others continue for months.

Scientists do know that pressure and heat build up underground until they can no longer be held back. Then boiling hot magma breaks through the earth's crust. It may explode into the air like balls of fire; or spray in all directions, like flaming rain; or ooze up slowly, like red-hot molasses. Once it is exposed to air, this molten rock is called lava. Lava may be thick and slow moving, or so thin that it runs over the ground like water.

As lava moves over the countryside, it causes great damage. But in many cases the greatest destruction is caused, not by the lava, but by the suffocating gases, smoke, and heat given off by the volcano. Other dangers are mud slides, choking dust, falling rocks, and fires.

The eruption of Washington State's Mount Saint Helens in 1980 came almost without warning. It had been inactive for one hundred twenty-three years—so long that people did not think much about it erupting again. But when it did, it destroyed huge forests and much wildlife. The volcanic ash it spewed out covered the ground like a gray, powdery snow that stretched for many miles.

The eruption of Mount Saint Helens was frightening and destructive, but like a pop-gun—compared to the cannon that was Krakatoa. This volcano is located on an island in the western Pacific Ocean. When it exploded in 1883, the sound could be heard thousands of miles away! And the dust rising from Krakatoa's crater drifted around the world three times.

Pumice, a kind of light stone often created by eruptions, covered so much of the sea that ships were not able to sail through parts of the Pacific Ocean. And the violent tsunamis that followed Krakatoa's thunderous eruption drowned more than thirty-five thousand people on other islands in the Pacific.

Volcanoes and earthquakes can be frightening and devastating. Yet in their awesome power, they are also uniquely beautiful. They remind us that the forces of nature are continually reshaping the surface of our earth. And scientists continue to study them—to listen for tremors that may signal a major earthquake and to watch for the awakening of another of the earth's sleeping volcanoes.